# *Puppies*

## 2025 CALENDAR

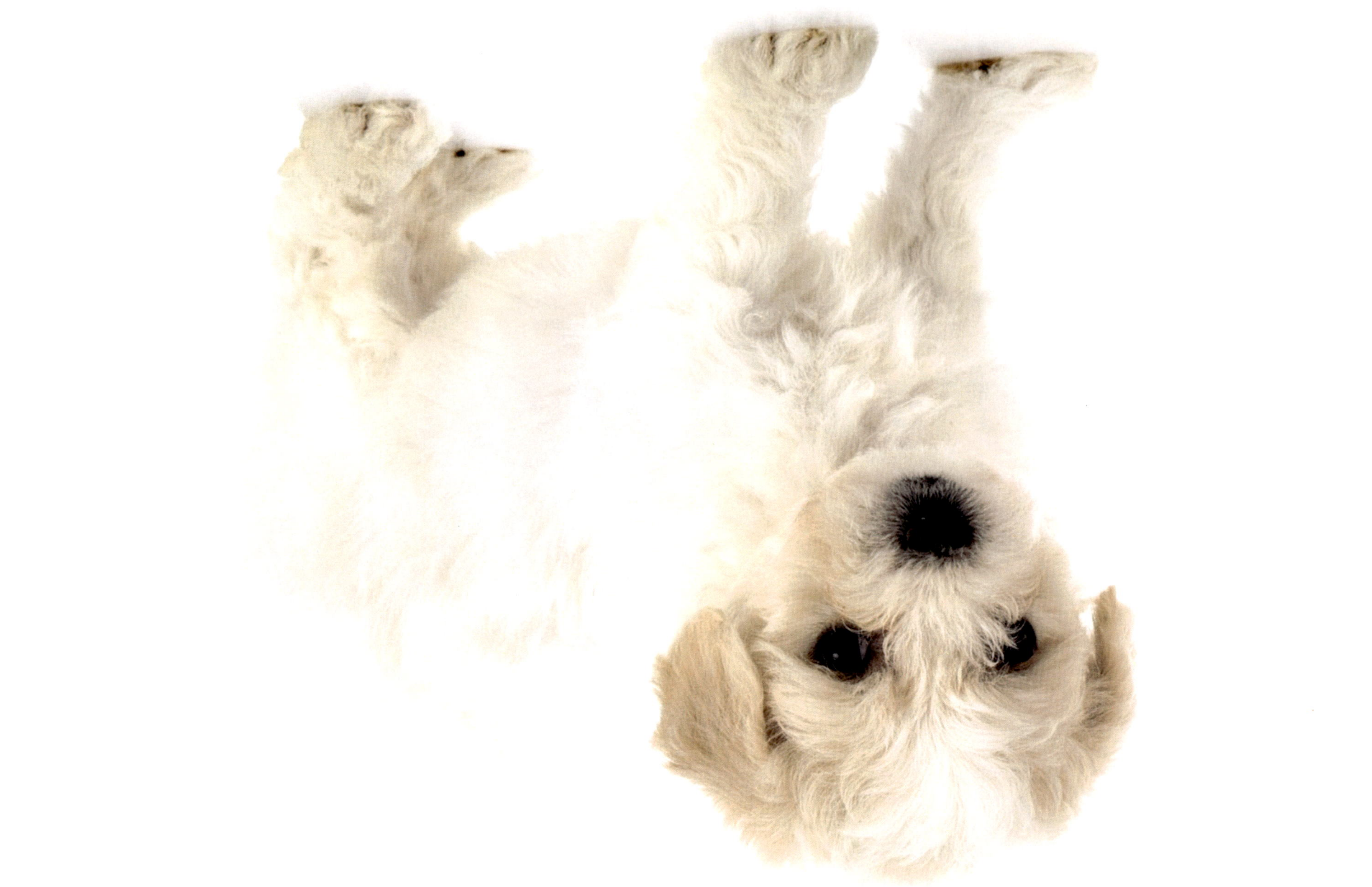

# JANUARY 2025

| SUNDAY | MONDAY | TUESDAY | WEDNESDAY | THURSDAY | FRIDAY | SATURDAY |
|---|---|---|---|---|---|---|
| 29 | 30 | 31 | 1 | 2 | 3 | 4 |
| 5 | 6 | 7 | 8 | 9 | 10 | 11 |
| 12 | 13 | 14 | 15 | 16 | 17 | 18 |
| 19 | 20 | 21 | 22 | 23 | 24 | 25 |
| 26 | 27 | 28 | 29 | 30 | 31 | 1 |

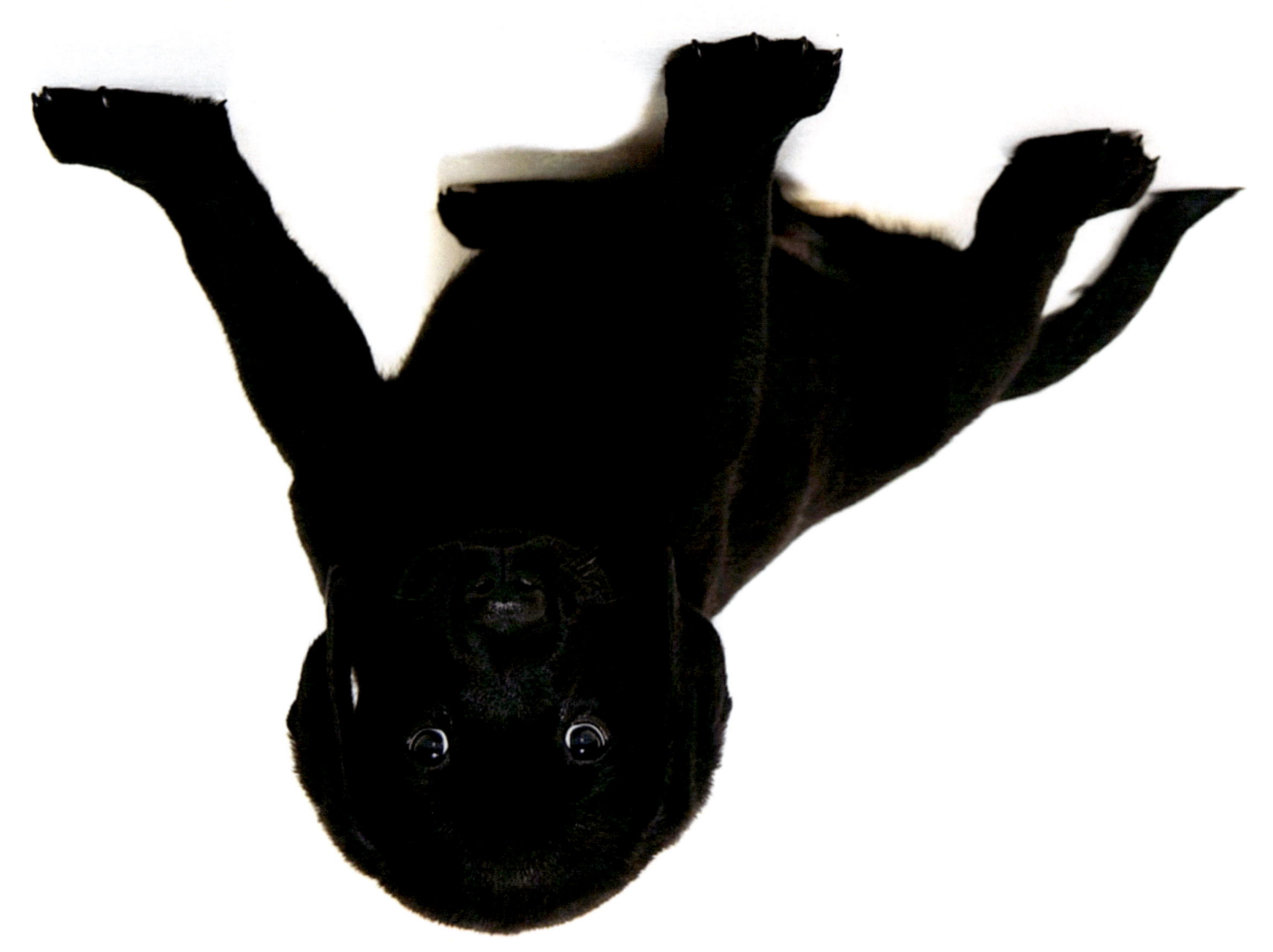

# FEBRUARY 2025

| SUNDAY | MONDAY | TUESDAY | WEDNESDAY | THURSDAY | FRIDAY | SATURDAY |
| --- | --- | --- | --- | --- | --- | --- |
| 26 | 27 | 28 | 29 | 30 | 31 | 1 |
| 2 | 3 | 4 | 5 | 6 | 7 | 8 |
| 9 | 10 | 11 | 12 | 13 | 14 | 15 |
| 16 | 17 | 18 | 19 | 20 | 21 | 22 |
| 23 | 24 | 25 | 26 | 27 | 28 | 1 |

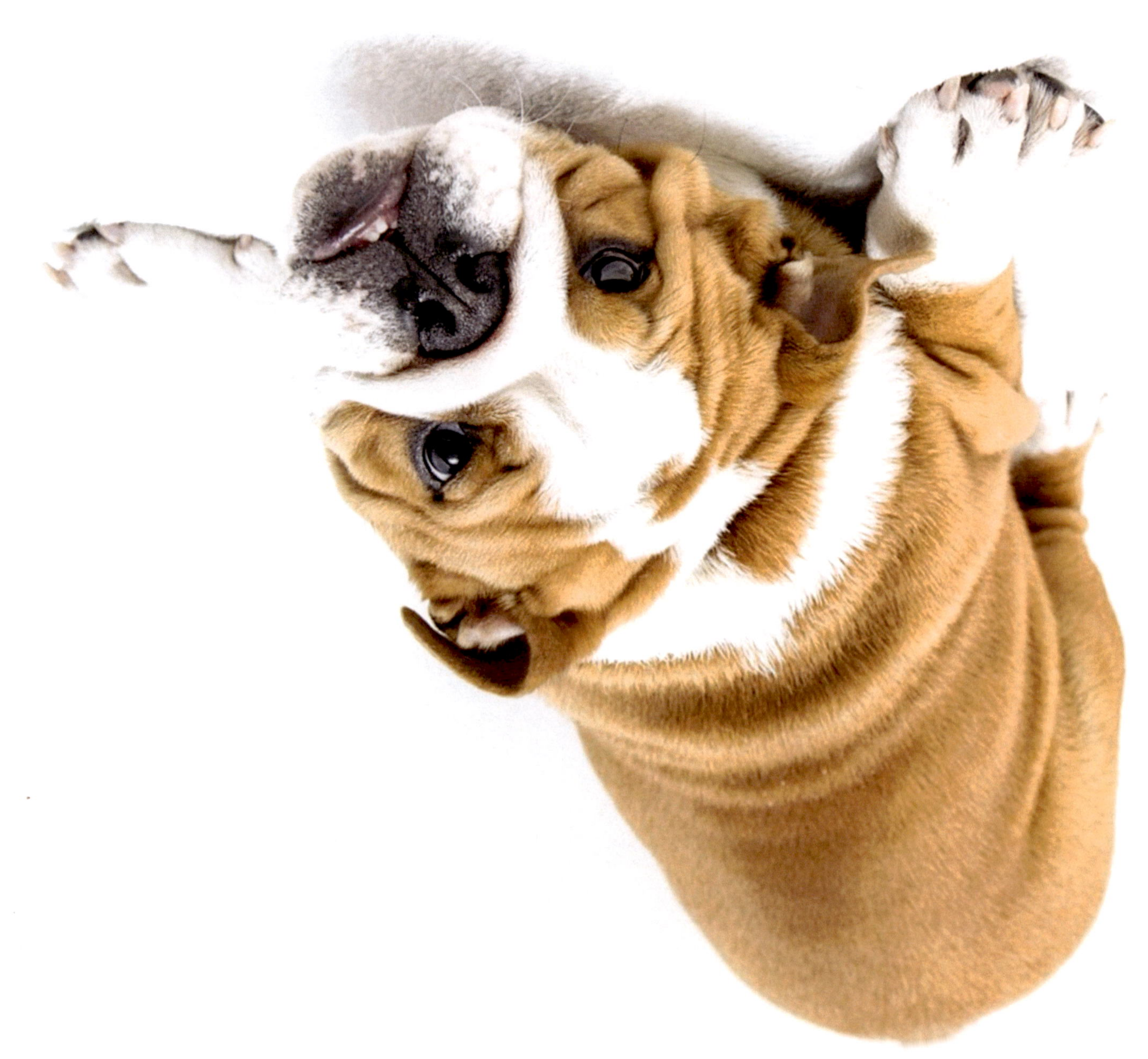

# MARCH 2025

| SUNDAY | MONDAY | TUESDAY | WEDNESDAY | THURSDAY | FRIDAY | SATURDAY |
|---|---|---|---|---|---|---|
| 23 | 24 | 25 | 26 | 27 | 28 | 1 |
| 2 | 3 | 4 | 5 | 6 | 7 | 8 |
| 9 | 10 | 11 | 12 | 13 | 14 | 15 |
| 16 | 17 | 18 | 19 | 20 | 21 | 22 |
| 23 / 30 | 24 / 31 | 25 | 26 | 27 | 28 | 29 |

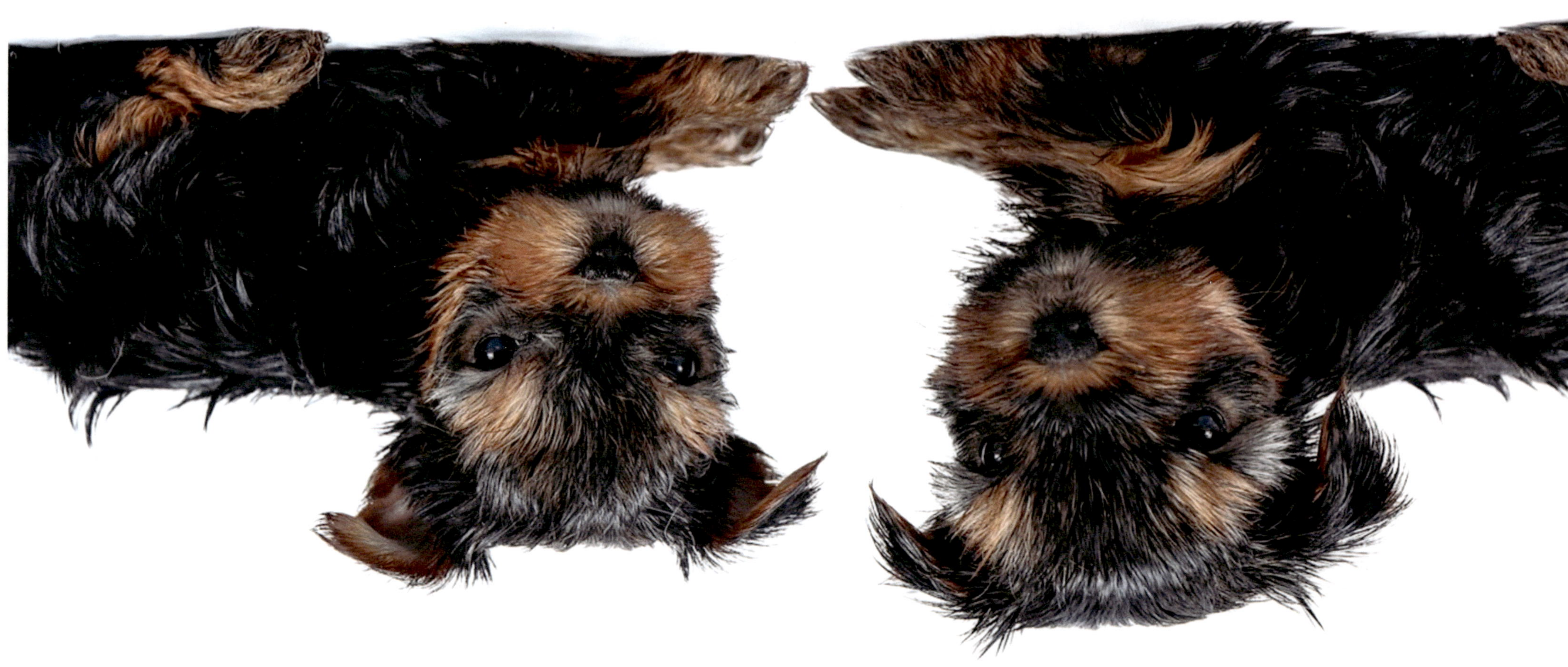

# APRIL 2025

| SUNDAY | MONDAY | TUESDAY | WEDNESDAY | THURSDAY | FRIDAY | SATURDAY |
| --- | --- | --- | --- | --- | --- | --- |
| 30 | 31 | 1 | 2 | 3 | 4 | 5 |
| 6 | 7 | 8 | 9 | 10 | 11 | 12 |
| 13 | 14 | 15 | 16 | 17 | 18 | 19 |
| 20 | 21 | 22 | 23 | 24 | 25 | 26 |
| 27 | 28 | 29 | 30 | 1 | 2 | 3 |

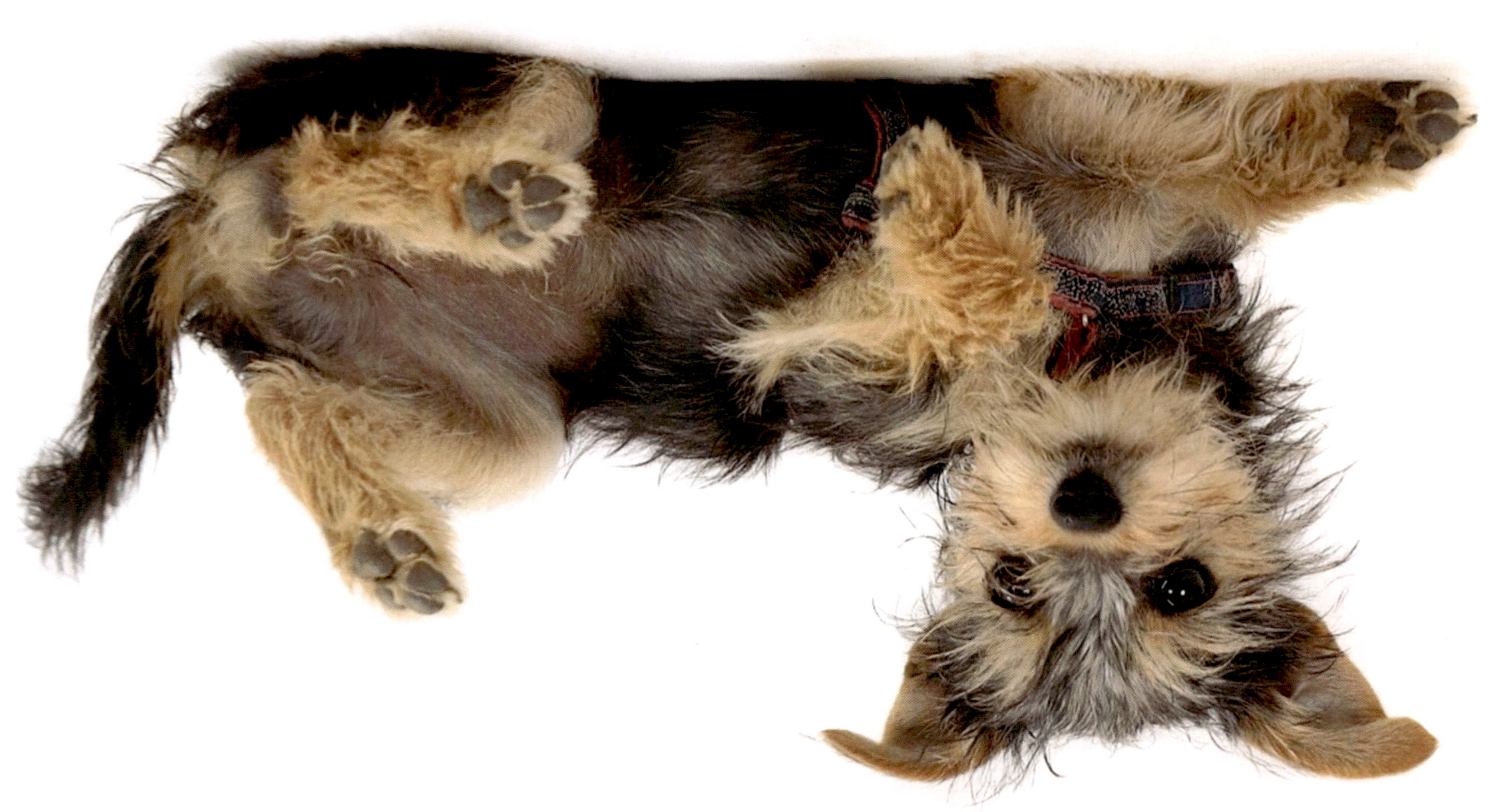

# MAY 2025

| SUNDAY | MONDAY | TUESDAY | WEDNESDAY | THURSDAY | FRIDAY | SATURDAY |
| --- | --- | --- | --- | --- | --- | --- |
| 27 | 28 | 29 | 30 | 1 | 2 | 3 |
| 4 | 5 | 6 | 7 | 8 | 9 | 10 |
| 11 | 12 | 13 | 14 | 15 | 16 | 17 |
| 18 | 19 | 20 | 21 | 22 | 23 | 24 |
| 25 | 26 | 27 | 28 | 29 | 30 | 31 |

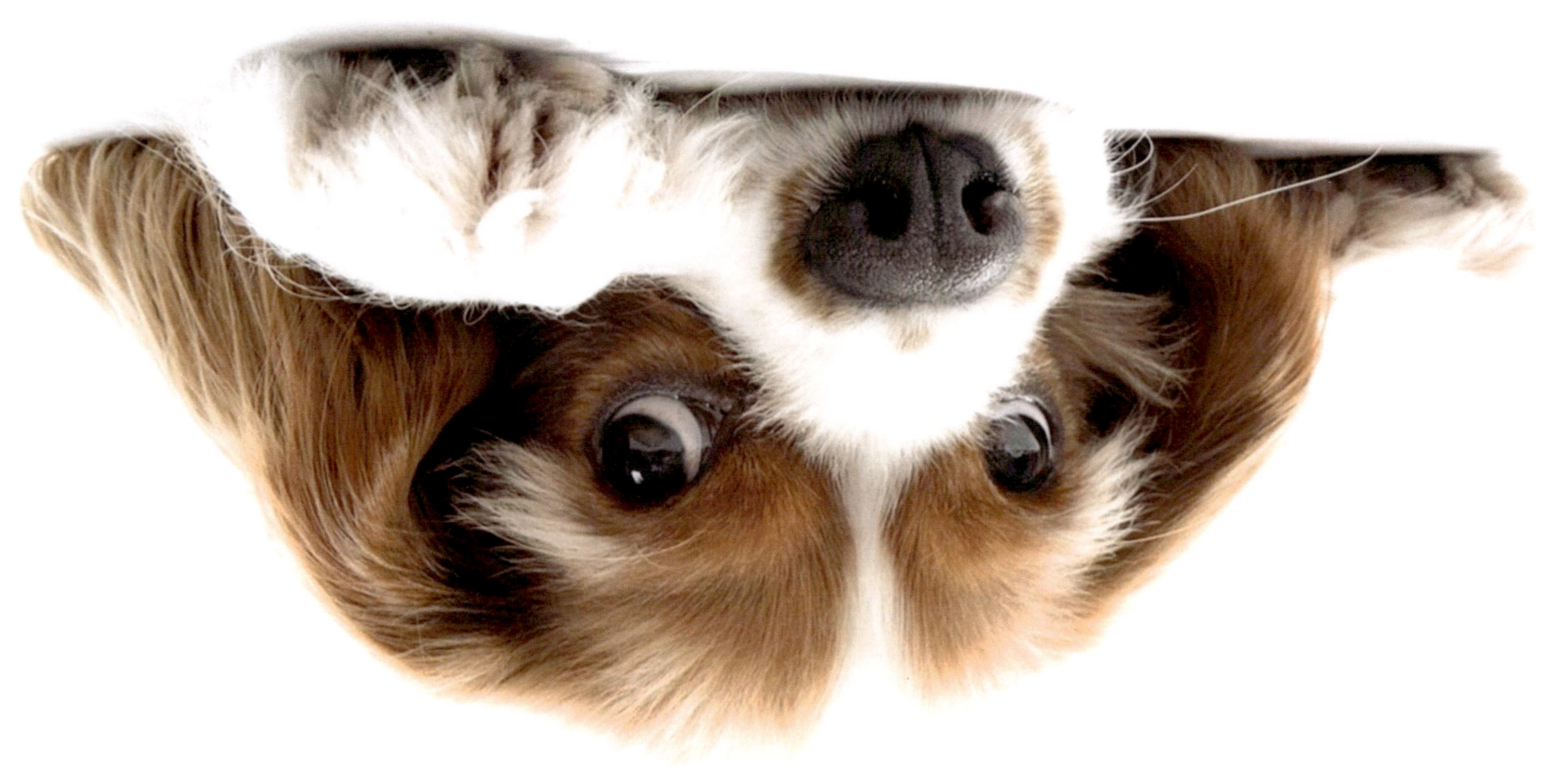

# JUNE 2025

| SUNDAY | MONDAY | TUESDAY | WEDNESDAY | THURSDAY | FRIDAY | SATURDAY |
|---|---|---|---|---|---|---|
| 1 | 2 | 3 | 4 | 5 | 6 | 7 |
| 8 | 9 | 10 | 11 | 12 | 13 | 14 |
| 15 | 16 | 17 | 18 | 19 | 20 | 21 |
| 22 | 23 | 24 | 25 | 26 | 27 | 28 |
| 29 | 30 | 1 | 2 | 3 | 4 | 5 |

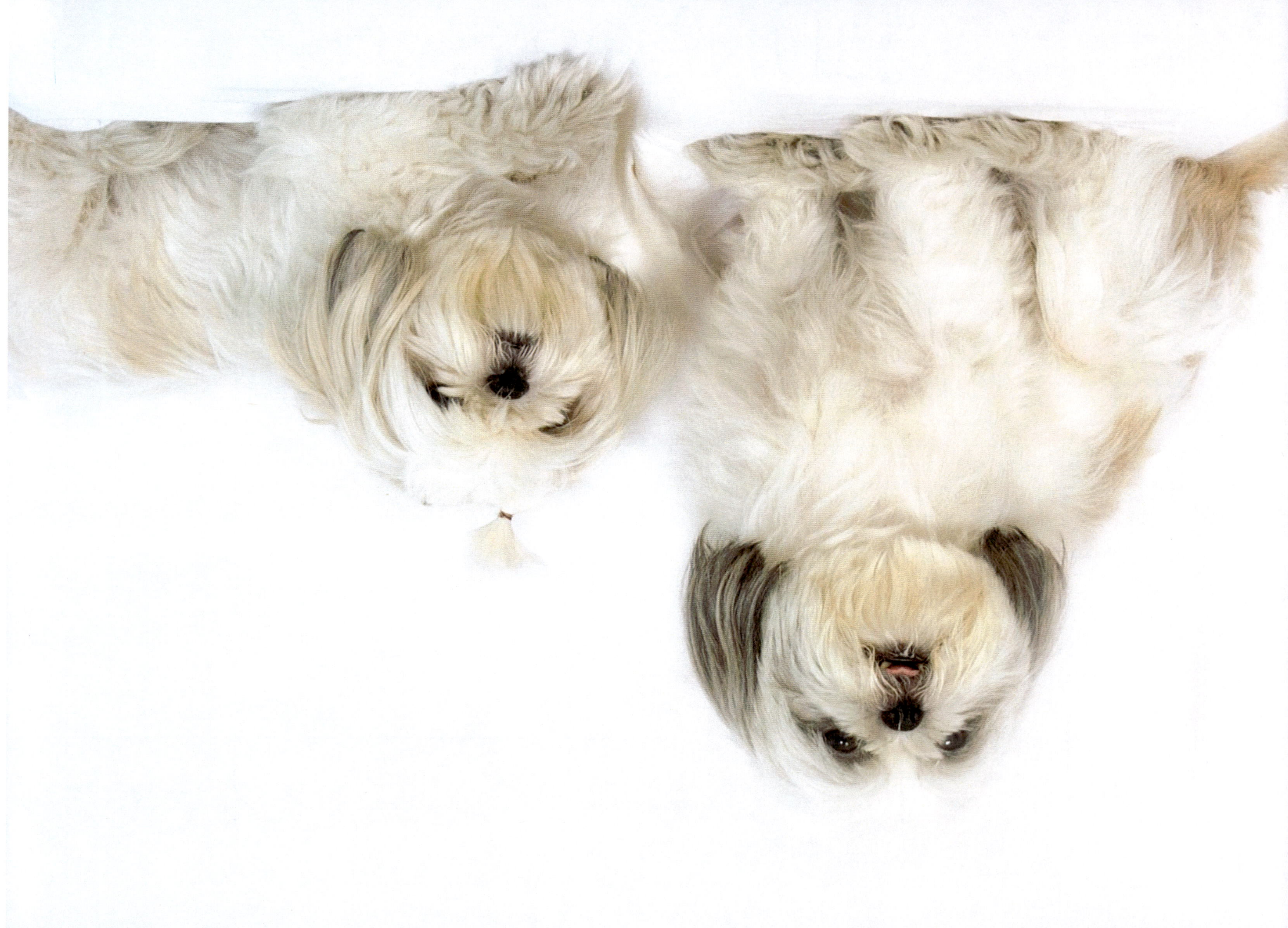

# JULY 2025

| SUNDAY | MONDAY | TUESDAY | WEDNESDAY | THURSDAY | FRIDAY | SATURDAY |
|--------|--------|---------|-----------|----------|--------|----------|
| 29 | 30 | 1 | 2 | 3 | 4 | 5 |
| 6 | 7 | 8 | 9 | 10 | 11 | 12 |
| 13 | 14 | 15 | 16 | 17 | 18 | 19 |
| 20 | 21 | 22 | 23 | 24 | 25 | 26 |
| 27 | 28 | 29 | 30 | 31 | 1 | 2 |

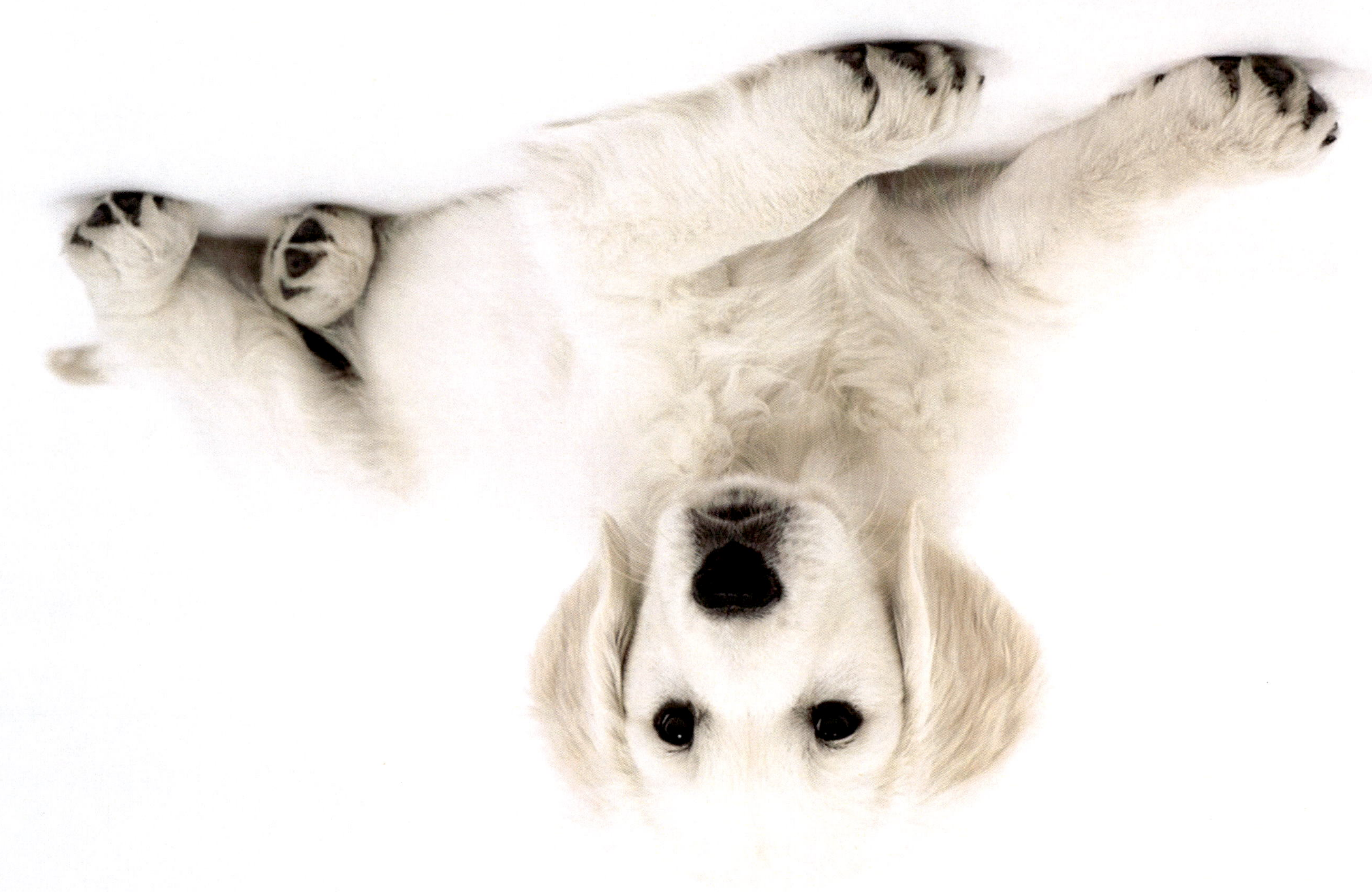

# AUGUST 2025

| SUNDAY | MONDAY | TUESDAY | WEDNESDAY | THURSDAY | FRIDAY | SATURDAY |
|---|---|---|---|---|---|---|
| 27 | 28 | 29 | 30 | 31 | 1 | 2 |
| 3 | 4 | 5 | 6 | 7 | 8 | 9 |
| 10 | 11 | 12 | 13 | 14 | 15 | 16 |
| 17 | 18 | 19 | 20 | 21 | 22 | 23 |
| 24 / 31 | 25 | 26 | 27 | 28 | 29 | 30 |

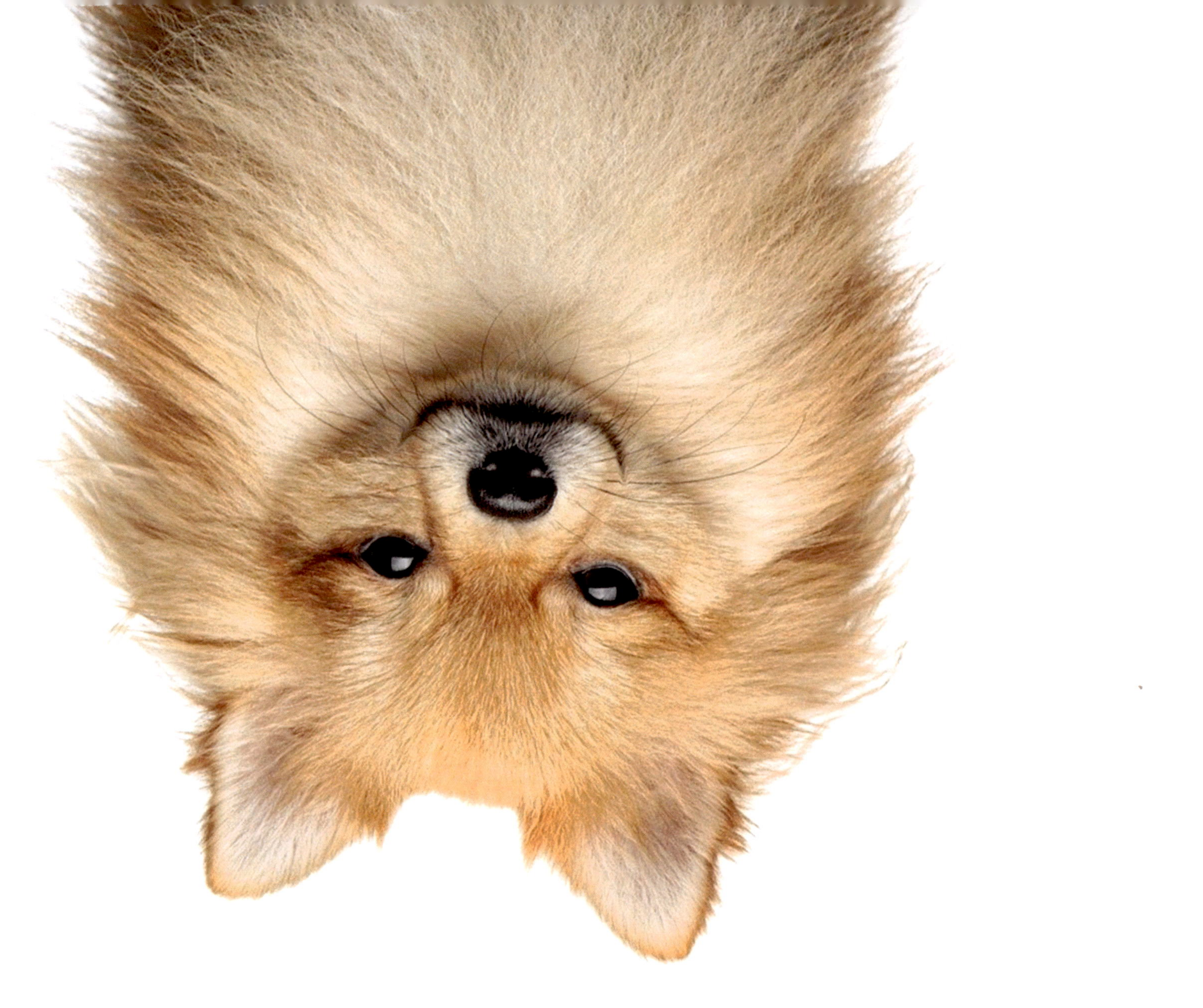

# SEPTEMBER 2025

| SUNDAY | MONDAY | TUESDAY | WEDNESDAY | THURSDAY | FRIDAY | SATURDAY |
|---|---|---|---|---|---|---|
| 31 | 1 | 2 | 3 | 4 | 5 | 6 |
| 7 | 8 | 9 | 10 | 11 | 12 | 13 |
| 14 | 15 | 16 | 17 | 18 | 19 | 20 |
| 21 | 22 | 23 | 24 | 25 | 26 | 27 |
| 28 | 29 | 30 | 1 | 2 | 3 | 4 |

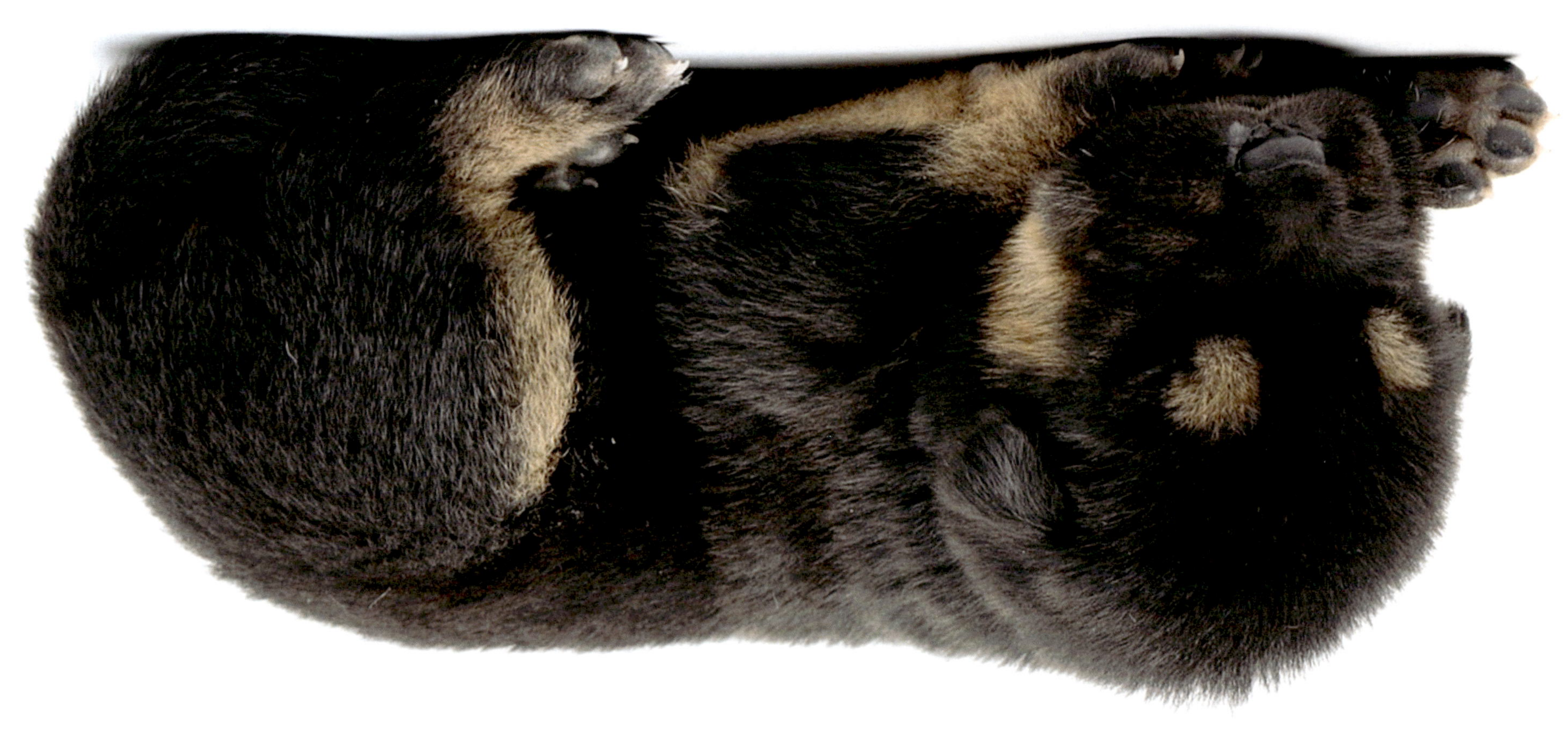

# OCTOBER 2025

| SUNDAY | MONDAY | TUESDAY | WEDNESDAY | THURSDAY | FRIDAY | SATURDAY |
| --- | --- | --- | --- | --- | --- | --- |
| 28 | 29 | 30 | 1 | 2 | 3 | 4 |
| 5 | 6 | 7 | 8 | 9 | 10 | 11 |
| 12 | 13 | 14 | 15 | 16 | 17 | 18 |
| 19 | 20 | 21 | 22 | 23 | 24 | 25 |
| 26 | 27 | 28 | 29 | 30 | 31 | 1 |

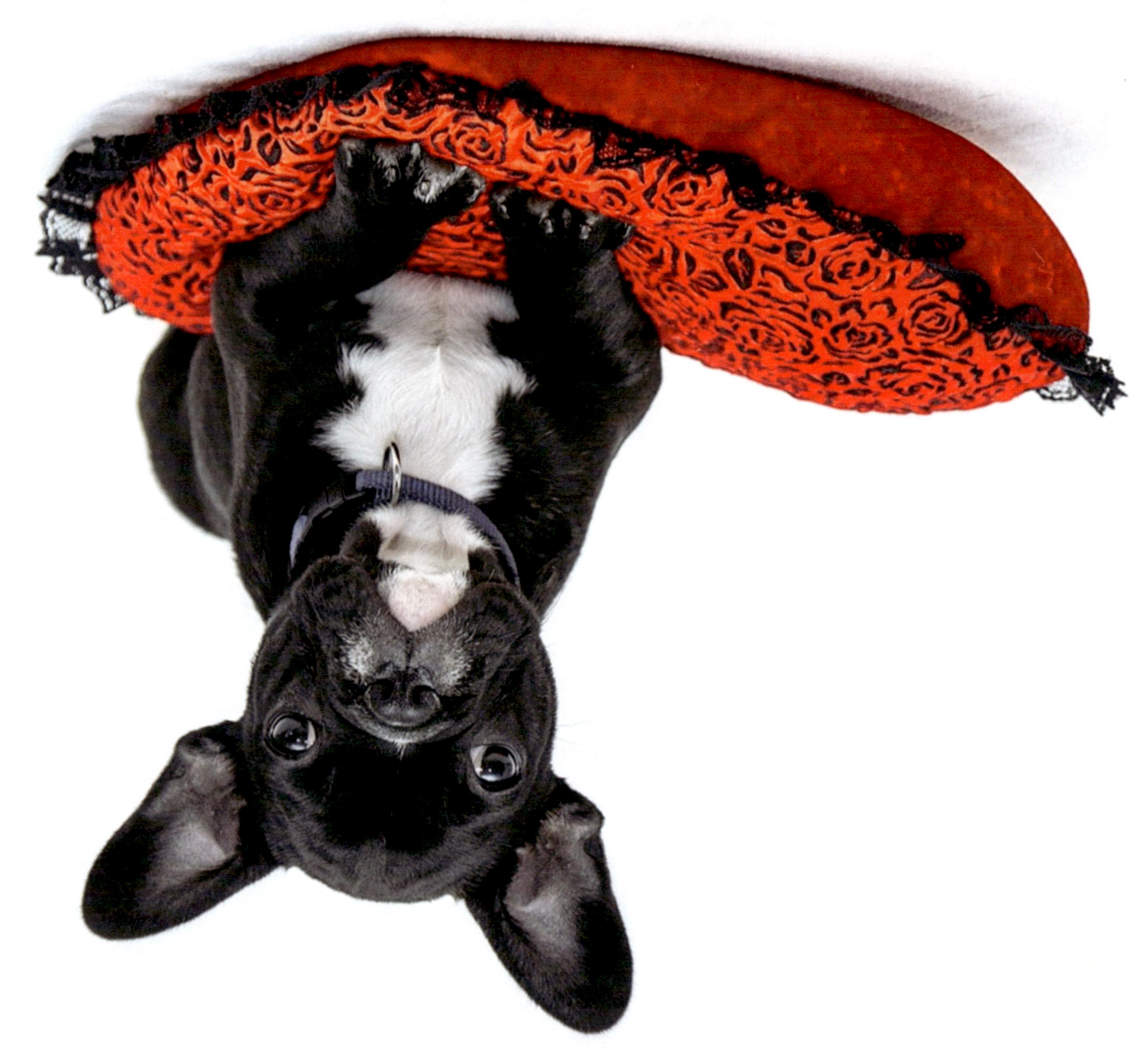

# NOVEMBER 2025

| SUNDAY | MONDAY | TUESDAY | WEDNESDAY | THURSDAY | FRIDAY | SATURDAY |
|--------|--------|---------|-----------|----------|--------|----------|
| 26 | 27 | 28 | 29 | 30 | 31 | 1 |
| 2 | 3 | 4 | 5 | 6 | 7 | 8 |
| 9 | 10 | 11 | 12 | 13 | 14 | 15 |
| 16 | 17 | 18 | 19 | 20 | 21 | 22 |
| 23 / 30 | 24 | 25 | 26 | 27 | 28 | 29 |

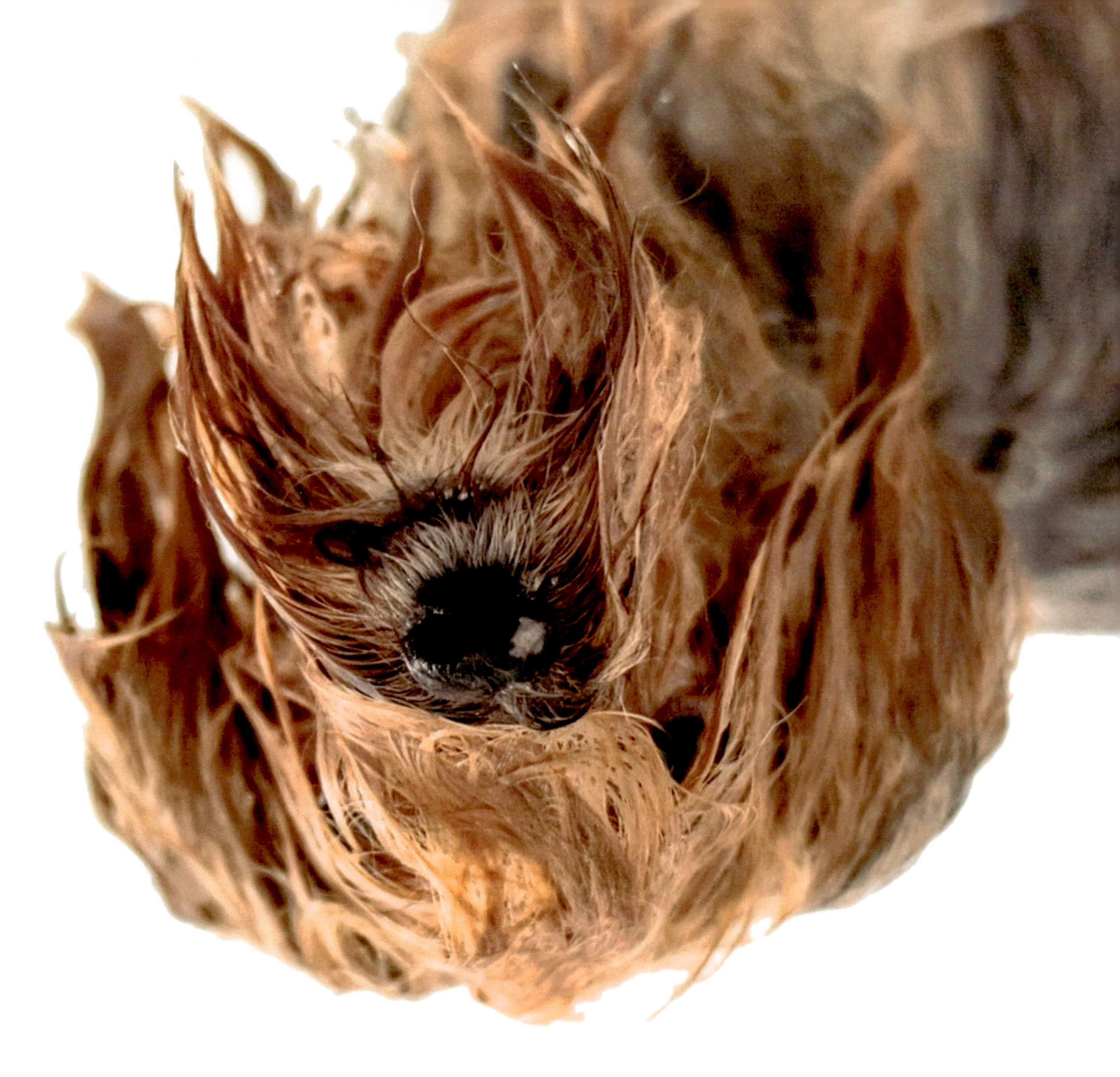

# DECEMBER 2025

| SUNDAY | MONDAY | TUESDAY | WEDNESDAY | THURSDAY | FRIDAY | SATURDAY |
| --- | --- | --- | --- | --- | --- | --- |
| 30 | 1 | 2 | 3 | 4 | 5 | 6 |
| 7 | 8 | 9 | 10 | 11 | 12 | 13 |
| 14 | 15 | 16 | 17 | 18 | 19 | 20 |
| 21 | 22 | 23 | 24 | 25 | 26 | 27 |
| 28 | 29 | 30 | 31 | 1 | 2 | 3 |

# The Top 30 Smartest Dog Breeds

(in order from smartest at the top)

Border Collie
Poodle
German Shepherd
Golden Retriever
Doberman Pinscher
Shetland Sheepdog
Labrador Retriever
Papillon
Rottweiler
Australian Cattle Dog
Pembroke Welsh Corgi
Miniature Schnauzer
English Springer Spaniel
Belgian Tervuren
Schipperke
Belgian Sheepdog
Collie
Keeshond
German Shorthaired Pointer
Flat-Coated Retriever
English Cocker Spaniel
Standard Schnauzer
Brittany
Cocker Spaniel
Weimaraner
Belgian Malinois
Bernese Mountain Dog
Pomeranian
Irish Water Spaniel
Vizsla

# Tips To Potty Train Puppies

1. Establish a Routine
Regular Feeding Schedule: Feed your puppy at the same times each day to regulate their digestive system.
Consistent Potty Times: Take your puppy outside at regular intervals, including first thing in the morning, after meals, and before bedtime.
2. Choose a Designated Potty Spot
Same Location: Take your puppy to the same spot each time. The consistent smell will encourage them to go.
3. Use a Crate
Crate Training: Use a crate that is just big enough for the puppy to stand up, turn around, and lie down. Dogs naturally avoid soiling their sleeping area.
4. Positive Reinforcement
Praise and Treats: Immediately reward your puppy with praise, treats, or playtime when they go potty outside.
5. Supervise Your Puppy
Constant Supervision: Keep an eye on your puppy when they are not in their crate to prevent accidents. Use baby gates to confine them to one area if needed.
6. Recognize Potty Signals
Behavioral Cues: Watch for signs that your puppy needs to go, such as sniffing around, circling, or whining, and take them outside promptly.
7. Avoid Punishment
No Scolding: Do not punish your puppy for accidents. Instead, clean up accidents with an enzymatic cleaner to remove all traces of odor.
8. Take Them Out Frequently
Frequent Breaks: Young puppies need to go out often. As a rule of thumb, take your puppy outside every hour, and more frequently if they are very young.
9. Use a Command
Potty Cue: Use a consistent verbal cue like "Go potty" or "Do your business" when taking your puppy to their designated spot. Over time, they will associate the command with the action.
10. Be Patient and Consistent
Consistency is Key: Stick to the training routine and be patient. Puppies learn at different rates, and consistent training will eventually pay off